He's been doing it all day ref!

A RANDOM HOUSE BOOK
published by Random House New Zealand
18 Poland Road, Glenfield, Auckland, New Zealand

www.randomhouse.co.nz
www.rugbyspeak.com

First published 2006. Reprinted 2006 (three times)

National Library of New Zealand
Cataloguing-in-Publication Data

Brown, Justin, 1973-
Rugby speak : classic rugby sayings / Justin Brown.
ISBN 1-86941-795-X
1. Rugby union football terminology.
2. Rugby union football humor.
3. New Zealand wit and humor 21st century.
I. Title.
796.3330207—dc 22

ISBN-13: 978 1 86941 795 6
ISBN-10: 1 86941 795 X

Text and cover design: Trevor Newman
Printed in China by Everbest Printing Co.

RUGBY SPEAK

Justin Brown

RANDOM HOUSE
NEW ZEALAND

RUGBY
SPEAK

CONTENTS

Justin Brown
is the author of
UK ON A G-STRING,
a book inspired by a lost
bet at a rugby game.
TEED OFF IN THE USA
soon followed. He
lives at the foot of
a volcano with
his family.

Dedication
Full credit to the
many players, coaches
and refs who
contributed

INTRODUCTION

Too often when
I'm at a rugby match, I don't
know what to yell out. Although, being a
Kiwi, I feel as though I should yell something.
Something informed, yet witty. Something that could be
used in the company of both yobbos and NZRU executives.
(And no, they're not the same thing.) So here it is:

RUGBY SPEAK

A book you can pop in your pocket along with your hip
flask and pull out should you ever feel the need to
yell out appropriate abuse from the terraces.

Rugby grammar

Research done on American football fans has proven that yelling and cheering for your favourite team while they are playing on TV has no effect whatsoever on the outcome of the game.

Course, things are different when you're yelling from the stand at a *live* match.

And although some rugby nuts like to watch test matches by themselves, at home, as though this solitary act of devotion will somehow make the players perform better, you really can't beat the sounds, smells and spirit of the real deal.

There aren't many rules when it comes to rugby grammar, but the following are paramount if you intend to sound at least a tad informed.

The referee is always abbreviated to 'Ref'. If you were to politely say 'Oh, Referee, I can see your point of view, but surely given the circumstances of the situation, that last call should be put forward for discussion at a later date', you'd probably be escorted from the ground.

The personal pronoun 'him' is always pronounced ''em', as in 'Get 'em!', 'Smash 'em!' and 'Nail 'em!'

Your team's players are always called by their first name or nickname, unless they're having a really bad game, when it's OK to use their surname — kind of like when you were naughty as a child and your mother used your full name. The opposition players are *always* called by their surname.

Remember, some comments are best made quietly to friends seated next to you, rather than shouted out. If in doubt, don't say it. You may lose all the credibility you have been trying to build up.

Note: Every game has its Sheryl and Barbs — the two old friends who haven't seen each other since the kids were at school. These fans are normally seated behind you and will talk about everything *but* rugby. Throughout this book you'll hear them pop up, just as you would at a game; normally, it must be said, when you're trying to focus on what is actually happening on the field.

What to say during the game

'Go you good thing!'

Recently adopted thanks to commentators at Fox Sports in Australia.
It'll go down even better if you can say it with an Aussie twang.

'Don't kick it, pass it!'
'Don't pass it, kick it!'

Together these cover most situations.

'Support! Come on, where's the support?!'

If we had to pay royalties for overuse of rugby slang,
I'd be poor thanks to this saying.
It's all I ever say at a game. Lazy? Yes. Ill-informed? Damn right.

'Get in there ya mongrels!'

Every team has its purse-carrying nancy boy. In my soccer team it was me.
Should you spot an absurdly clean winger, who when not plane-watching
is sponging his sprigs mid game, yell this at him.

To be used when you see a bunch of grown men huddled together,
all moving forward slowly, eyeing the ground as if one has lost a contact lens.

Just one of many heckles from the terraces that works a treat.
Course, having a blow-up sheep at your disposal adds to the authenticity.
Fire it into the air and watch it dance around the terraces.

'Bring back Buck!'

Refers, of course, to the great Buck Shelford. Screaming out this cracker never fails; it can even be used at cricket, netball and soccer matches to add humour should your team be on the end of a grand whipping.

'Feed the backs!'

A classic saying and one that features in Fred Dagg's song, *We don't know how lucky we are*. Means 'Give the ball to the fast dudes at the back who run like cheetahs, not to the potbellies up front who couldn't run a piss-up in a brewery.'

'Pin your ears back and go!'

Quite how any player would a) have time to do this or b) have the necessary skills to do so is beyond me, but that doesn't stop it being a favourite from the sideline. Off the field it's also handy if you ever run into Prince Charles.

'Oh, get off the grass you poofter!'

The actuality of both teams achieving such a feat would result in no game at all. This saying is normally directed at a 'love to hate' player who has tripped over his own feet and claimed a penalty.

'Carlos Spencer, take a bow!'

Again, a recent addition courtesy of the callers at Fox Sports in Australia. Note: it's 'bow' as in 'to bend the body in respect', not as in 'weapon for shooting arrows' or the 'fore-end of a ship'. If either of the latter appear in view, you're at the wrong sort of event altogether.

'Sit down in front!'

Every crowd has its over-enthusiastic seat hopper. Every ten seconds this individual stands up, as if this will somehow get him closer to the action. He wouldn't do it at the movies — don't let him do it at the rugby.

'Oh get up, you great ponce!'

Normally directed at some Aussie who looks as though he's suffering a life-threatening injury. No one in their right mind would play on, but yelling this at least keeps the said player honest.

You little beauty!

Many uses:
1) When your team scores.
2) When the beers arrive.
3) When a rotten nectarine hits the 'sit down in front' guy.

Oh, you biiiooooooddy idiot!

Even I know when a player's been handed a try on a platter, only to drop the ball metres before the line. This call won't cheer him up — but will make you feel better.

Simple really. If your team has more points than the other — but only just — and time is up, scream this at the showpony who wants to score one last try. Chances are, if he doesn't kick it out, he'll drop the ball, the other team will score and he'll get beaten up on his way to the changing room. And on his way to the car park. And his wife will leave him because he won't be in the team next week and consequently won't be buying that new three-piece leather lounge suite. See, it's just easier to kick it out.

'Take the three!'

If there's a penalty right in front of the sticks —
otherwise known as the posts,
or if you're really new to the sport,
the big white H — it's best to kick
for goal and take the three points.
(Similar to banking your money in Monopoly.)

'Does your boyfriend play?'

An absolute classic to yell out just after a player has dropped a complete sitter and is standing on the wing, holding back the tears and seriously considering finishing his BA given he won't be offered that lucrative Japanese club deal.

'Man in front!'

A rather strange adage. Still, better than
'Man on top' or indeed 'Man from behind.'

'Call that man
a taxi!'

The politest thing you can yell at a player who has thuggishly punched someone right in front of the ref and has been sent off. Don't literally *call* him a taxi as in 'You're a taxi.' That's just childish.

'Mark your man!'

Not an invitation to go and take a leak on him. Refers to choosing your opposite number and irritating the hell out of him the entire game.

'Play for time!'

The on-field equivalent of clock-watching at work. While the office worker surfs dodgy websites and waits for 'beer o'clock', the rugby player flirts with the ball, passes it around the team and performs a premature ceremonial dance until the ref blows the final whistle.

'Thanks for coming!'

The perfect salt-in-the-wound comment after
your opposition has just been thrashed.

'Hunt the pigskin!'

Back in the eighth century the English used to cut the head off a Viking and hoof it around the park. Although all agreed this was a good laugh, they didn't fight enough battles to provide enough new 'balls' to keep the troops entertained. Some genius then decided to cut the bladder out of a dead cow and use that. This is why the air-filled rubber bag inside the ball is called a 'bladder'. But cow bladders used to burst before half-time. To make them stronger, they covered them with animal skins, namely cowhide, deerskin, goat hide, and eventually, and most successfully, pigskin.

'Take it up the fat man's track!'

The said player can't run wide, can't run fast, and doesn't care too much for moving at all. For him, the best route is straight up the middle — otherwise known as the fat man's track.

'Run it up the guts!'

See above.

It's a crucial
point in the
game.
The ref's
gone upstairs
with it.
It's all tied
up here
with three
minutes to
play.

Barbs
'Oh, I love your shoes!'
Sheryl
'What, these old things?
You'll never guess what
I paid for them!'
Barbs
'What?'
Sheryl
'Bargain. Guess!'
Barbs
'I don't know.'
Sheryl
'Guess!'
Barbs
'I really don't know.'
Sheryl
'Guess!'

'Come on, you've got them rattled!'

Despite its optimistic tone, this is usually yelled out when your team is losing by over a hundred points. You'd have to be a complete idiot to believe this if you were actually on the winning team.

'Goose step, à la David Campese!'

Imagine being confronted by an angry goose or swan. Now put a rugby ball under its arm and a Wallaby shirt on its back and you've got David Campese, the man who played over a hundred games for Australia, scored 64 international tries and perfected the run of a web-footed bird.

'Tackle, Red, tackle!'

Oh, come on, even I know this one.

'Spread it! Spin it out!'

Get the ball out to the backs and wingers. After all, they've been waiting for the bloody thing all afternoon and they're tired of signing autographs.

'Orene Ai'i, you know what your problem is, don't ya? Too many vowels, not enough consonants!'

Used for Auckland winger Orene Ai'i if he's having a shocker.

'Oh, that's gotta hurt.'

The only thing better than watching players smash into each other like a couple of duelling wildebeest is watching the replay on the big screen. 'Oh, that's gotta hurt' is normally followed by 'Oh, nasty!'

Tight head!

Doesn't refer to your mate at the bar who won't get the beers in (he's a tight arse). This is one to use when the blokes are huddled together looking for the contact lens [see 'Drive! Drive! Drive!']. When the opposition halfback feeds the ball into the scrum and your team gets it, that's a tighthead. Quite a coup in the game of rugby — akin to seeing a white rhino in Greytown.

Don't kick it straight to 'em!

Take his legs!

Even though it may be more desirable to take his wallet, or indeed his girlfriend, his legs, for now, will have to do. At least he won't be troubling the scorers any time soon.

'Play the whistle!'

Although many players (namely me) would be more at home playing the triangle, or indeed the fool, doing the old 'Roger Whittaker' refers to playing on until the ref actually blows his whistle, instead of just stopping mid-match when it seems like the ref might blow his whistle.

'Wipers kick!'

Angled kick across the field, like the angle of a windscreen wiper.

'Straight over the black dot!'

Some things take a long time to discover but once you do you wonder why you never noticed them before. Kind of like when you buy an Audi and think yours is the only one on the road. Until you go for a drive. I'd never noticed the black dot between the goal posts on a rugby field before — now I see it every time.

What to say to the ref

It's fair to say that most comments directed at the ref aren't exactly complimentary. However, this doesn't stop it being the favourite pastime of many a rugby follower. Besides, there's really something special about yelling 'You're as blind as a bat!' then hiding behind a six-foot, man-eating ogre in the crowd. A lot of abuse directed at the ref is self-explanatory — or kept simple enough so he'll at least understand it.

'He's been doing it all day, ref!'

Perhaps the most favoured call of all. Even if the offending player hasn't been doing it all day — indeed, if this is the first time he's ever played the game — this saying cannot fail. Yell it out willy-nilly: at church, at the pub — you'll win a friend every time. Only 'Bring back Buck' is used more often.

'About bloody time, ref!'

Half-brother of — and can be used directly after — 'He's been doing it all day, ref'.

'Read the bloody rules, ref!'

Though it's hard to believe, referees are only human. Often, when they're supposed to be focusing on the offside or forward pass, they're really thinking about shoe sales and chocolate brownie recipes. This is a classic heckle should the ref be making more wrong calls than Don King's hairstylist.

Sinbin!

Yellow card!

Said player has done something bad.

Red card!

Real bad.

'Stick the whistle up your bum, ref!'

I haven't made this up. Colin, a good friend of mine and an ex-ref was hurled this corker during a club game.

'Stick your whistle where the sun don't shine!'

This could have been the same game. I'll have to ask Colin.

'Where's your
guide dog, ref?'

'That was a knock-on,
you bifocalled bastard!'

'I know where the ref's
staying, the Copthorne
by the airport!'

'Did you get a whistle for Christmas, ref?'

'You're blowing the whistle with your arse!'

I heard this one from a not-entirely-sober supporter in the South Stand at Eden Park during a 2005 Lions match. He had obviously tired of clever, well-informed comment. Why be astute when crassness gets just as big a laugh?

It's all right fellas, you're playing sixteen men!

To be used when it's blindingly obvious that the ref has not called one decision in your team's favour all afternoon.

'Not straight, ref!'

Without jumping to any conclusions, most players on the rugby field are straight. However, this refers to the ball being thrown into the lineout.

'That's forward, ref!'

If you're not aware that the ball's not allowed to be passed forward in rugby, you should really be at the basketball. Or the movies. Anywhere but a rugby stadium. For your health's sake.

Offside, offside!

I asked my uncle what 'offside' meant. Here's what he said:

'In open play, players are offside if they are either in front of a team-mate who is carrying the ball, or in front of a team-mate who has kicked the ball. Offside players cannot participate in any further part of the game until they become onside again. If offside players do participate in the game, for example by playing the ball or obstructing an opponent (by loitering) then their team will be penalised. In any other part of play (scrums, rucks, mauls or lineout), players are offside if they are in front of the offside line. This is an imaginary line parallel to the goals which runs through the hindmost foot of the hindmost player in the ruck/maul/scrum. Any player joining a ruck/maul or scrum from in front of the offside line is offside and their team will be penalised. At a lineout only players in the line (normally seven per team), both half-backs and both hookers are allowed within 10 metres of the line. The remaining players must be more than 10 metres away from the line or they will be penalised. They may only move after the ball has been caught and the catching player has his feet on the ground. Got it?'

'No,' I replied. 'And you've got something in your teeth.'

That's
a bad
mistake.
There
were many
outside
him.
He could
have
passed it.

Barbs
'Patrick's putting
two words together
now.'
Sheryl
'Really, is he walking
yet?'
Barbs
'No, nearly.'
Sheryl
'Jacob's almost
running now. But he
was an early crawler
as well . . .'

'You need new glasses, ref!'

'We know where you live, ref!'

'He's lying all over the ball, ref!'

One would think, in a game like rugby, it would be all right to lie all over the one thing both teams have been chasing all afternoon. But sometimes, when you're lying on top of the ball (and none of your team members are in sight), you've got to let the other team have a go. Even if it is your cricket set.

'He was on his feet, ref!'

One would think being 'on your feet' was a prerequisite if you intended on getting anywhere. If you are on your feet — as opposed to lying down and hogging the ball — the good news is you're allowed to hold onto the ball till the cows come home. Or at least till the rest of your team arrives.

'Good decision, ref!'

For every 50/50 decision that goes your way.

'Aw, ref!'

For every 50/50 decision that goes the other way.

'Watch your back, ref!'

Could be directed at the ref when the opposition is offside behind him, to which he'll probably reply, 'Watch your mouth.'

'Off! Off! Off! Off!'

A good call should the crowd have been pushed to the absolute limit. Often the game is just better off if the ref leaves.

What to say when you're sitting next to the old man in the stand who's been to every game since 1922

Not only has George been to every home game, every away game and every Third XV game since the year dot, he's also a veritable fount of rugby knowledge. But be warned, he doesn't suffer fools gladly. (All the more reason why I never sit next to him.) The only way to impress George is to offer an array of rugby witticisms and hope like hell he doesn't see you delving into this book while he's looking for his teeth. The following should work a treat:

'He couldn't catch a cold.'

'He couldn't kick the skin
off a rice pudding.'

'He's like a robber
in the night.'

'He couldn't fight his way
out of a wet paper bag.'

Every rugby game sports a No. 8 who looks like a cross between Bilbo Baggins and King Kong. This is appropriate abuse whenever he drops the ball.

He's found his true position on the wing.

He's playing out of position, that's why.

'It doesn't matter what we say — it's a try in tomorrow's paper.'

'Straight in the bread basket and straight out again.'

This should only be said when a player has caught the ball . . . then dropped it. And in the process pissed off a nation and deflated its economy overnight.

'That's a hospital pass.'

Let's imagine you play rugby but don't like getting hit, tackled, smacked or thumped. Hence, when you receive the ball, the first thing you do is throw it to someone else — anyone else! — to avoid getting hurt. Now imagine Bubba, the biggest mother on the field, is running straight at you and is about to eat your scrawny white butt for breakfast. At the last second you pass the ball to some poor bloke who doesn't have time to react before he himself is annihilated. As a result, you get off scot-free, Bubba beats his chest and your team-mate gets a free ride in an ambulance.

129-4

'That's a cricket score.'

If the team you're playing has more than three numbers in their score, that's bad. Real bad.

'They're lucky they're not playing the Boks. You can't play like that against them.'

'They didn't play like that in my day.'

Probably not appropriate to say to someone who was born before your parents, but what the hell, it sounds nostalgic. And old dudes love nostalgia — although they say it's not what it used to be.

'Play the tramlines.'

Nickname for 'sidelines'. (Can often be heard on commentary —
'Oh, he's gone straight up the tramlines!')

'He's playing out of his skin.'

The said individual is having a great game and
smiling because later he'll be getting laid.

'It's all about the top two inches.'

They say the best sportsmen are those who can read a game by using the top two inches. Unlike some footballers who prefer using the bottom six. Or am I being a little generous?

'That's not a ruck, that's a maul.'

Not entirely true — a ruck's a ruck, a maul is where you go shopping.

'He'll be warming the bench at this rate.'

'The first five's had an armchair ride.'

Some days your bus is early, there's a morning tea shout followed by a long, boozy lunch, you find $20 in your jacket pocket and your boss is fired for surfing porn. The above is the equivalent for the first five on the rugby field.

'Let's just hope they go the full 80.'

'Keep it low into the wind.'

'He was all over that
one.'

'This test isn't gonna be
won on tries. It's kicks
that win a game.'

'The game's won up front.'

'It's a ten-point wind.'

'Rain is a great leveller.'

'That one's got snow on it.'

Can be used when the ball is booted high into the air. Also known as the big up-and-under or a 'Garryowen', after an Irish club —Garryowen — that used it frequently.

'First-up tackles are vital.'

'Got to score first in the second half.'

Even if their team is losing by 50 points, most coaches are under the illusion that if they score first after half-time, the game will be theirs. Trust me, it won't.

'Form is temporary;
class is permanent.'

'I could have
done that.'

Only to be used when the try scored looks particularly easy.

'My grandmother could have made that tackle.'

'We're playing at home — might as well add ten points.'

There's something to be said for sleeping in your own bed and knowing which drawer the teaspoons go in. No touring team, however, has this luxury. Perfect reason, then, to whinge about hotels, local food and abusive crowds, then, come Saturday, to lose by at least ten.

'Oh, there's a bit of how's-your-father. He's given him a couple of don't argues and Bob's your uncle. Look at the claret coming out his cauliflowers.'

There's a fight . . .

'It's all on for young and old!'

It's still going . . .

Bring on the paramedics.

'He's had to go off into the blood bin.'

This was not around in the time of Colin Meads, Buck Shelford and Kevin Everleigh. Now, though, at the first sign of claret players have to go to the blood bin. This has come about since the discovery of AIDS.

They've got numbers out on the right.

Amazingly, most players also have numbers on their backs. The above, though, is typically muttered with a good dollop of excitement when a try is imminent, due to the throng of players on the wing. Unless you play for Italy.

'I taught him everything he knows.'

Penalty
given
away.
There's
a chance
for points
here.
It's a five
metre
scrum.

Sheryl
'So, who should have been
voted off then?'
Barbs
'The pretty boy.'
Sheryl
'But he's my favourite!'
Barbs
'He can't dance!'
Sheryl
'He doesn't have to!'
Barbs
'No, it was all over
for him the minute he
took his shirt off . . .'

How to state the bleeding obvious

Given that I know less about rugby than most, I was astonished (while living in England) to be asked to do radio commentary for Bath Rugby Club. Their reasoning was that I was a New Zealander — and New Zealanders know *everything* about rugby. But not this one.

Admittedly, becoming a commentator was every boy's dream come true, including mine. In reality, though, it was an unmitigated disaster. I knew nothing about rules, positions, offsides, mauls and rucks. This was to become hopelessly apparent when I was sent to Bordeaux to call the Heineken Cup final. To this day I feel sorry for the poor folk back in Wiltshire who had to endure my ill-informed warblings. For when I wasn't copying — word for word — what the Sky TV team next to me were saying, I was howling, 'Number 8 . . . to number 7 . . . to number 15 . . . to number 4 . . . TRY!'

Remember, though, just because a commentator says it doesn't mean it's OK for you to. It's your choice whether to use the following clangers at a game but beware, you'll have to live with the consequences. Fellow supporters may look at you sideways or they may consider you a genius. There's a fine line.

It's all about the ball. You can't win without the ball.

If you don't score points, you don't win.

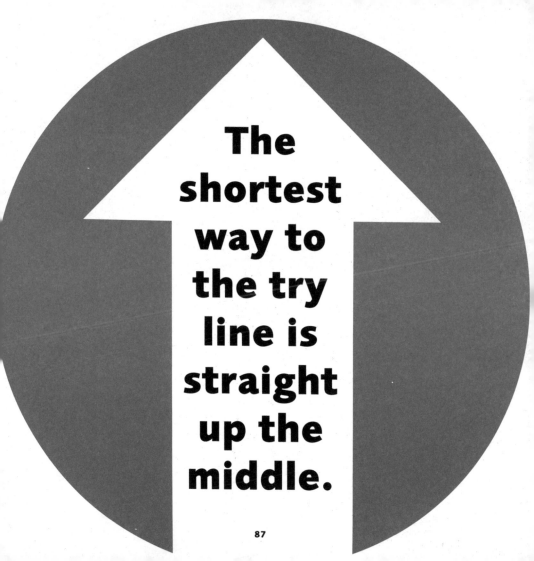

The shortest way to the try line is straight up the middle.

'He's a better player when he's on the field than when he's on the bench.'

'It's who's in front at the end that counts.'

'He loves running with the ball.'

He's such a good player on his feet.

That's a
dodgy
tackle in
anyone's
book.
The ref's
reaching
for his
pocket.
Will it
be red or
yellow?

Barbs
'What did they pay for it?'
Sheryl
'Seven hundred.'
Barbs
'Seven hundred?
It doesn't even have a view!'
Sheryl
'I know, and they've gone
unconditional.'
Barbs
'What's the GV?'
Sheryl
'Five forty.'
Barbs
'Oh, why didn't they just
wait?'
Sheryl
'You know what Joy's like,
gotta have it now . . .'

Things women shouldn't say

'Is there anything on Sky Movies?'

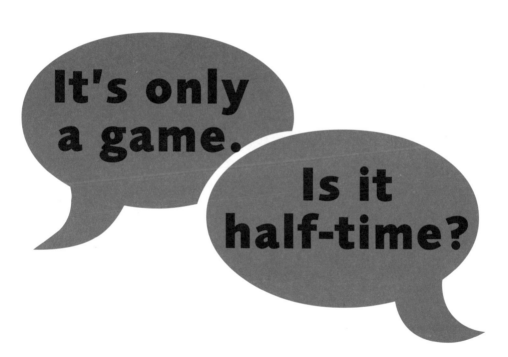

'Which colour are
we again?'

'I like the other colour
better, it's prettier.'

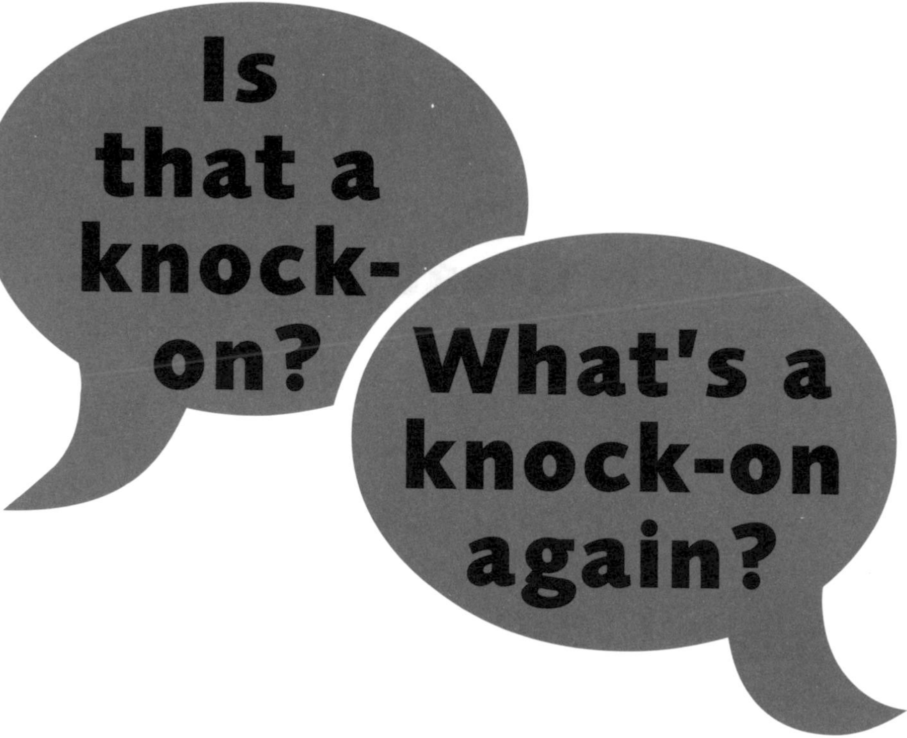
Is that a knock-on?
What's a knock-on again?

'He's cute.'

'Oh, he's got nice eyes.'

'Great arse.'

'Look at those thighs!'

'I love their short
shorts.'

The
lineout's
been
stolen.
He's
cleared
the ball.
A try
could
on from
here.

Sheryl
*'What are
you doing for
Christmas?'*
Barbs
*'Not much,
Darren's mother's
staying again.'*
Sheryl
*'Again! Bloody hell,
how many years
in a row is that
now?'*
Barbs
'I've lost count.'
Sheryl
*'Oh well, she'll be
dead soon . . .'*

Things that sound rude but aren't

'Ruck it!'

Not to be confused with

**'Ruck you,' 'Ruck off' or
'I couldn't give a flying ruck.'**

'Ruck 'em, ruck 'em!'

'They're feeling each other out.'

'He's holding the ball in the wrong hand when he runs.'

You should always hold the ball in two hands.

Don't let him get inside you!

'Ball's out, ball's out, ball's out!'

'It's under the hooker's feet, ref!'

'Go on, have
a quickie!'

'They're not
blowing over
the ruck.'

'I knew
they'd come
out hard.'

'You don't like to see hookers going down on players like that.'

'He's looking for some meaningful penetration into the backline.'

It's getting sloppy out there. There's a bit of dew on the ground tonight. The slippery ball's made going tough.

Sheryl
'You'll never guess what!'
Barbs
'What?'
Sheryl
'I've finally found a way to make the kids eat cauliflower.'
Barbs
'Really! God, I don't think Jack's eaten a single vegetable in six months . . .'

'The first-five's running across field calling out, come inside me, come inside me!'

'I don't like this new law, because your first instinct when you see a man on the ground is to go down on him.'

'There's nothing that a tight forward likes more than a loosie right up his backside.'

'He has a habit of creaming players at the ruck.'

'They're going to have a look upstairs to see if he was interfered with.'

'It's OK,
you're allowed to screw the scrum.'

Advanced rugby speak

Beware!

If you're a beginner, this section is not for you. Stick to the shallow end until you have your waterwings.

I reckon they should try the grubber. If that fails, give the chip, droppie or torpedo a whirl. Then again, a drop punt or up-and-under could do the trick. Oh, wait a minute, the tighthead's not square! Is that the loosehead boring in?

Chances are some of this will make sense to somebody. Just be sure to say it quickly, and if challenged, reply in Spanish. Or fake a heart attack.

'Is he playing fly half?' 'Yeah, outside half.' 'Or stand-off?' 'Yeah, first five.' 'Don't you mean pivot?' 'Yeah.'

Rather confusingly, these all mean the same thing. Use any term and you'll gain brownie points. Typically, though, the fly half/outside half/stand-off/first five/pivot is the guy who kicks a lot, runs a lot and appears in lots of undies ads.

'Oh come on, truck and trailer!'

Sadly, if you don't have the ball you can't just push through and take out players.

'There's a big blind to play with.'

Kids love playing with blinds, especially two-year-olds, who find them particularly useful for trying to strangle younger siblings. A blind on the rugby field refers to the blindside, which is the narrower side of the field at a set play, ruck or maul. See, I told you it was confusing!

'They're too high
in the mauls.'

'They're not hitting the
rucks hard enough.'

They're not clearing out at ruck time.

They've created the extra man.

'Look for the elaborate triple scissors move involving the second five and the fullback.'

'The home side has called the tune in the line-outs.'

He's
kicked
it deep.
There's
a man
under it.
Bounce
is cruci
here.

Barbs
*'Really? I thought
he'd moved out.'*
Sheryl
'No, he stayed.'
Barbs
*'He got his end
away with that slag
from the office and
she let him stay!'*
Sheryl
*'She had to, Barbs,
she's never
mowed a lawn in
her life. She doesn't
know how to do the
banking or the bills
or anything.'*

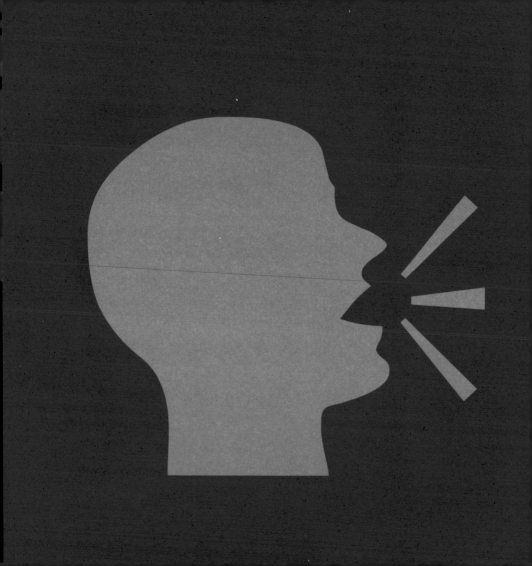

What to say after
the game

8

'Oh well, back to the drawing board.'

'We're rebuilding for the World Cup.'

'Either side could have won.'

'What a difference a week makes.'

'I'm really proud of the boys.'

'We gave it our best.'

'Full credit to the opposition.'

First perfected by former All Black captain Sean Fitzpatrick.

It's a game of two halves.

A New Zealand cliché that takes the cake. Although now used as a joke,
for years this was used quite seriously in interviews.
Inspired a TV show of the same name.

'I think they've picked the strongest squad available.'

'No stone has been left unturned.'

Thanks to the ladies for the spread.

If you have any classic sayings you'd like to share — be they rugby, cricket or netball — please email them to sayings@rugbyspeak.com for possible inclusion in future collections.

For more classic rugby sayings, check out www.rugbyspeak.com

Special thanks to Rob Appleyard, Adrian Drew, John McCarten, Colin Nicholls, Brian Sharp and Paul O'Brien.